uncapped

EMBRACE THE ADVENTURE

Lighting the Fire Within
100 Days of Walking With God

Uncapped
Embrace the Adventure

Uncapped Series © 2018

Lighting the Fire Within:
100 Days of Walking With God © 2018

CJ Tetley
M. Abrokwah

To our families and those who inspired us to walk with God.

The Uncapped Story

It was late winter 2018. Spring was right around the corner, which was supposed to be welcome news in this part of the world, especially for us, CJ and Mike. It had been a long winter, both physically (the cold had overstayed its welcome) and spiritually. We were both staring down a long dreadful year ahead. The stress of life and our individual meandering walks with God had taken a toll on our meagre attempt at New Year resolutions.

I, CJ, had just been through the most difficult season of my life. Our family was going through the stress of health challenges, accidents, and then I lost my job. All of these circumstances led me on a quest for new meaning in life. A new adventure; something beyond the mundane. Something intriguing and inspiring. I was looking for something that would take my relationship with God and my impact on my world, to another level. I could see the potential for greatness in my family and friends who had settled for mediocrity in their lives. This bothered me. I desperately wanted to help them and I had many ideas but, often found myself facing dead ends. I was praying, seeking and studying the scriptures and was unaware of how God was going to answer my prayers. Something just had to be different, I kept telling myself.

I, Mike, was fighting through a dry season of life. In one of my writings, I coined that season "my desert years" (okay, perhaps a little dramatic). I later called it "my season of loss" (definitely more accurate). Like CJ, even in the midst of my frustration and uncertainties and perhaps as a result of these, I was loaded with ideas, striving to forge forward but feeling capped and trapped. I couldn't figure out how to come out of the funk so I started writing to clear my mind. Incidentally, and now I see God's tender hand of rescue, God was laying a hidden foundation. A couple of years prior, I had bought a few domain names. I was particularly excited about one of them: "uncapped.ca". At the time, I was walking alongside friends who were facing their own seasons of dormancy. I felt strongly about helping my friends uncap themselves - to breakthrough. I had ideas on some ways partnering with them to make that happen. I was unaware my own season was about to take a downturn. And when it did, for the life of me, I couldn't figure out how to take all that was swirling in my head and heart and use it to uncap myself.

Then one winter morning, everything changed in ways we could have never imagined. We had met to celebrate CJ's birthday. We both discovered how similar our journeys were. One conversation led to another as we shared openly about life, God, work, family and relationships. Our paths could not have been more identical. We were already bonded in friendship and in this conversation discovered not only our share seasons and quest through it, but also our love for writing. What was abundantly clear was that we both deeply desired to thrive and held an undying passion to influence lives for God.

We built each other up and resolved to push a little, just a foot or two beyond our comfort zone and enter where the magic happens: The Uncapped Zone!

That is when this shared desire to be uncapped was fanned into flames. This devotional book (and many more to follow) came out of that desire and the scriptures are a result of that journey which we aim to share with you.

Contents

Fanning the Flame:

How To Use The Book

His word is in my heart like a fire,
a fire shut up in my bones.
I am weary of holding it in;
indeed, I cannot.

Jeremiah 20:9(b) (NIV)

"Is not my word like fire," declares the Lord

Jeremiah 23:29(a) (NIV)

We want to light a fire in your heart for God. We want you to dream about your life again.

That's the ultimate goal of this book. Throughout the bible when men and women were connected with God they became limitless in their power and uncapped in what they were able to accomplish. Their stories continue to inspire people all over the world. So what was the purpose behind their stories? Simply to be read as historical text or interesting information? No! Their stories were written to inspire your faith in God and to motivate you to take action in your own life.

You see, God wants to walk with you and to write

your story of faith with you.

Amazing things happen when we are filled with God's Spirit and His Word. They become the fabric of our being and the overflow of our hearts. As the prophet Jeremiah described in the scriptures above, when God's word is in your heart it lights a fire within you that you will not be able to contain. You will be filled with so much power, joy and excitement for God that you will want to share it with everyone. And your fire, or your faith, will spread to other people and inspire them to walk with God also.

Children are pure in heart and are boundless in their appetite for fun and excitement. What makes them unique from adults is their insatiable desire for discovery and ability to learn. They willingly take on new challenges because they want to experience life as an active participant. Of course they don't think about it in those terms. But that's what it is – "I want in!" In short, they love growing and experiencing life!

It is also true for adults. There is nothing more exciting or rewarding than taking on a new challenge and succeeding. Pushing yourself to limits that you never believed you were capable of reaching. You're guaranteed to boost your self-esteem while jam-packing your memory bank of victories born of acts of courage. Your victories mark your life as cornerstones of faith, courage and your potential for future success.

But for many of us, we stop taking on new challenges at some point and victories become distant memories. Instead, our personal expression of celebration becomes an extension of our favorite sports team or TV Show. We become passive participants in our own lives and people of minimal impact on the world around us. In short, we become "capped" at reaching our potential in both life and in our faith.

Many of the limits that we believe about our own potential were initially set by other people. They incorrectly minimized our potential by their wrong assumptions and shared these false beliefs with us. Their assumptions have become the limits we set for ourselves. These adopted false and limiting beliefs then stop us from taking any courageous steps towards learning, growing and taking on new adventures or challenges that would lead to personal victories. Equally worse, our faith in God becomes limited because we bring these crippling beliefs into our relationship with Christ (Mark 6:5-6). Then for years, we live in a state of mediocrity, never challenging or refuting the false limitations that we now believe about Christ and ourselves.

Today you can change this.

This reflective book is a starting point to ignite or reignite your faith in God. But, you need to light the fire in your heart again or start a fire that never existed. For this to happen, you need to be dedicated to spiritual training and discipline. It will take time. It will take effort. It will take commitment.

We want to encourage you to slow down a bit. To ponder the passage and the questions of the day and push beyond the norm to **Light The Fire Within**. We are inviting you to take a stand for your faith, decide to go deeper with God and ultimately with others.

Fires need fuel. The spiritual fire within you needs fuel too! The guidelines below are designed to help you use this book and the daily scriptures are prayerfully and thoughtfully chosen to "Fan the Flame" of spiritual fire in your life. The daily scriptures provided are short to highlight the specific focus of the chapter. The supporting questions will draw you into a deeper, personal study of God's Word and will further help you to grow in your relationship with God and with those around you.

Follow the steps for the next 100 days and watch the fire for God and a deep relationship with Him begin to grow within you. We want to impress upon you that as we have discovered in our own walk, to keep a fire burning you must continually add fuel. Your spiritual walk is no different. In order to keep your spiritual fire burning, you must put in the effort. No one can do this for you. Remember this, the time and effort that you put into your relationship with God will directly determine the strength and size of the spiritual fire within you.

Once you begin the process of writing down your answers to the questions provided, you will quickly notice a pattern. This is by design to strengthen your study of the scriptures. You may need to read additional verses that surround the scripture if this helps you.

So why all of the questions? To help you dig deep into your heart. Also, the old adage is true: practice makes perfect. The more you practice this pattern of reflecting, questioning and answering, the more aware, honest and intentional you will become in your walk with God.

You will notice that one question is repeated daily, "Who needs to hear this scripture?" This question is so important - don't skip it - answer it daily. It calls you to remember or even to memorize the passage and to spread the fire of God's word with someone who needs the encouragement or inspiration.

Fires will spread quickly if given the opportunity. If you take the time to do the work in this devotional, and share the scriptures and your insights with other people, you will inspire them to walk closer with God.

Our world is in a spiritual battle and we are God's soldiers. The battle is for the hearts and minds of every human being on our planet. We can all agree that whenever we make intentional decisions to grow, our lives, our families and the world will be transformed and uncapped!

The rewards of your efforts will be joy and lives changed for eternity.

Let's get started!

Hope

~

Luke 24:13-34

Day 1

3 And not only this, but we also exult in our tribulations, knowing that tribulation brings about perseverance; 4 and perseverance, proven character; and proven character, hope;5 and hope does not disappoint, because the love of God has been poured out within our hearts through the Holy Spirit who was given to us.

Romans 5:3-5 (NASB)

Day 1 – Fanning the Flame
Firestarter
Fuel for Fire: *Hope*

- ☑ We all go through trials in life. How well do you handle them?

- ☑ What is this scripture trying to teach you?

- ☑ What does "perseverance and proven character" mean?

- ☑ What can you do practically to make this scripture come alive in your life?

- ☑ What changes do you need to make?

- ☑ Who needs to hear this scripture?

Day 2

[10] *Be* devoted to one another in brotherly love; give preference to one another in honor; [11] not lagging behind in diligence, fervent in spirit, serving the Lord; [12] rejoicing in hope, persevering in tribulation, devoted to prayer, [13] contributing to the needs of the saints, practicing hospitality.

Romans 12:10-13 (NASB)

Day 2
Firestarter
Fuel for Fire: *Hope*

☑ What does it mean to "rejoice in hope"?

☑ What is this scripture trying to teach you?

☑ How does this scripture challenge you?

☑ What new insights about God have you learned?

☑ What can you do practically to make this scripture come alive in your life?

☑ Who needs to hear this scripture?

Day 3

11 I hope the Eternal, the God of your ancestors, makes you a thousand times more numerous and blesses you just as He said He would.

Deuteronomy 1:11 (VOICE)

Day 3
Firestarter
Fuel for Fire: *Hope*

☑ Read through the chapter for context. How does this apply to your faith?

☑ Where do you see hope in this scripture?

☑ How does this make you feel about God and the hope He has for you?

☑ Who needs to hear this scripture?

Day 4

15 But as for me, my hope is to see Your face.
When I am vindicated, I will look upon the *holy* face of God,
and when I awake, *the longing of* my soul will be satisfied in *the glow of* Your presence.

Psalm 17:15 (VOICE)

Day 4
Firestarter
Fuel for Fire: *Hope*

☑ What is the message of hope that the writer is trying to covey?

☑ Does this scripture move your heart? How?

☑ Would other people say that this scripture reminds them of your walk with God?

☑ What do you hope for in your relationship with God?

☑ Who needs to hear this scripture?

Day 5

7 Many put their hope in chariots, others in horses,
but we place our trust in the name of the Eternal One, our True God.

Psalm 20:7 (VOICE)

Day 5
Firestarter
Fuel for Fire: *Hope*

☑ Where is your hope today?

☑ How would you write a modern version of this scripture with your name included?

☑ Who wrote this scripture and what were the circumstances?

☑ How does this relate to you and your life?

☑ Who needs to hear this scripture?

Day 6

24 Be strong and let your heart take
courage,
All you who hope in the Lord.

Psalm 31:24 (NASB)

Day 6
Firestarter
Fuel for Fire: *Hope*

☑ Where do you need to be courageous in your life right now?

☑ What does it mean to "let your heart take courage"?

☑ What would happen in your life if you lived out your faith like this? Who would you be able to help?

☑ Does this describe your relationship with God? In what ways?

☑ Who needs to hear this scripture?

Day 7

¹⁸ There is surely a future hope for you,
and your hope will not be cut off.

Proverbs 23:18 (NIV)

Day 7
Firestarter
Fuel for Fire: *Hope*

☑ What do you hope for in the future? What is God's hope for you?

☑ What does "your hope will not be cut off" mean?

☑ Why is this proverb important in our lives?

☑ How does this scripture challenge your faith?

☑ Who needs to hear this scripture?

Day 8

18 But God will never forget the needy;
the hope of the afflicted will never perish.

Psalm 9:18 (NIV)

Day 8
Firestarter
Fuel for Fire: *Hope*

- ☑ How are you needy today? How are you afflicted?

- ☑ What have you experienced in your life that reminds you of this scripture?

- ☑ How can you apply this scripture to your life?

- ☑ Who needs to hear this scripture?

Day 9

³ No one who hopes in you
will ever be put to shame.

Psalm 25:3(a) (NIV)

Day 9
Firestarter
Fuel for Fire: *Hope*

☑ Write out your version of this scripture.

☑ How would you teach this scripture to other people? How would it help them to trust God?

☑ Does this describe your relationship with God?

☑ How does your hope in God need to grow? What changes do you need to make?

☑ Who needs to hear this scripture?

Day 10

Guide me in your truth and teach me,
for you are God my Savior,
and my hope is in you all day long.

Psalm 25:5 (NIV)

Day 10
Firestarter
Fuel for Fire: *Hope*

- ☑ What is God teaching you about hope currently?

- ☑ How is a person guided in God's truth?

- ☑ Why would the writer include the statement "for you are my God and Savior". How does this give you hope?

- ☑ What person in the bible does this scripture remind you of? Why?

- ☑ Who needs to hear this scripture?

Day 11

21 May integrity and uprightness protect me,
because my hope, Lord, is in you.

Psalm 25:21 (NIV)

Day 11
Firestarter
Fuel for Fire: *Hope*

☑ Write out your understanding of this scripture.

☑ How does this scripture give you hope?

☑ How is this biblical teaching different from ways of the world around us?

☑ Would other people say that this scripture reminds them of your walk with God? How?

☑ Who needs to hear this scripture?

Day 12

18 But the eyes of the Lord are on those
who fear him,
on those whose hope is in his unfailing
love.

Psalm 33:18 (NIV)

Day 12
Firestarter
Fuel for Fire: *Hope*

☑ What is this scripture trying to teach you?

☑ What does it mean to "fear" God?

☑ How does God provide unfailing love? How does this love give you hope?

☑ How can you apply this scripture to your life?

☑ Who needs to hear this scripture?

Day 13

20 We wait in hope for the Lord;
he is our help and our shield.

Psalm 33:20 (NIV)

Day 13
Firestarter
Fuel for Fire: *Hope*

☑ Often times God's protection is described as a shield. What is He protecting you from?

☑ Why do we need to "hope for the Lord"?

☑ What have you experienced that reminds you of this scripture?

☑ Who needs to hear this scripture?

Day 14

24 For in hope we have been saved,
but hope that is seen is not hope; for who
hopes for what he *already* sees?

Romans 8:24 (NASB)

Day 14
Firestarter
Fuel for Fire: *Hope*

☑ Write this scripture in your own words. What does God want you to know?

☑ What do you hope for in your life? What can't you "see" currently?

☑ Describe when you first put your hope in God. What did He do for you?

☑ How can you apply this scripture to your life?

☑ Who needs to hear this scripture?

Day 15

13 Now may the God of hope fill you with all joy and peace in believing, so that you will abound in hope by the power of the Holy Spirit.

Romans 15:13 (NASB)

Day 15
Firestarter
Fuel for Fire: *Hope*

    ☑ How does this passage give you hope?

    ☑ How does the Holy Spirit help you?

    ☑ How would you explain this scripture to someone else?

    ☑ How can you apply this scripture to your life?

    ☑ Who needs to hear this scripture?

Faith

~

Daniel 3:1-30

Day 16

17 When Abram was 99 years old, the Eternal One appeared to him *again, assuring him of the promise of a child yet to come.*

Genesis 17:1(VOICE)

Day 16
Firestarter
Fuel for Fire: *Faith*

- ☑ What is faith in God?

- ☑ What is Abraham's story of faith? Why is his story important to Christians?

- ☑ What promises did God make with Abraham? What promises did God make with you?

- ☑ Where is your faith today? How would other people describe your faith?

- ☑ What changes do you need to make?

- ☑ Who needs to hear this scripture?

Day 17

Eternal One: I am the God-All-Powerful. Walk before Me. *Continue to trust and serve Me faithfully*. Be blameless *and true.*

Genesis 17:1(VOICE)

Day 17
Firestarter
Fuel for Fire: *Faith*

- ☑ Who is God speaking to and how does this relate to faith?

- ☑ What do you want to accomplish with your faith?

- ☑ Who are your heroes in the faith and why?

- ☑ Where do you need to put more faith in your life?

- ☑ Who needs to hear this scripture?

Day 18

9 I want you to know that the Eternal your God is *the only true* God. He's the faithful God who keeps His covenants and shows loyal love for a thousand generations to those who *in return* love Him and keep His commands.

Deuteronomy 7:9 (VOICE)

Day 18
Firestarter
Fuel for Fire: *Faith*

☑ How is God faithful through His covenants?

☑ How are you faithful to God? How do you show God love?

☑ When have you experienced God's faithfulness?

☑ How are you teaching yourself and others God's commands? How does this connect with your faith?

☑ Who needs to hear this scripture?

Day 19

Make this your one purpose: to revere Him and serve Him faithfully with complete devotion because He has done great things for you.

1 Samuel 12:24 (VOICE)

Day 19
Firestarter
Fuel for Fire: *Faith*

☑ What is your purpose currently? Ask someone to describe your purpose as they see it.

☑ How does someone revere God? How about you?

☑ List all the great things God has done for you. How does this encourage your faith?

☑ Who needs to hear this scripture?

Day 20

The Eternal One rewards those who are faithful and righteous.

1 Samuel 26:23(a) (VOICE)

Day 20
Firestarter
Fuel for Fire: *Faith*

☑ What is this scripture trying to teach you?

☑ Why does God reward a person's faith and righteousness?

☑ Does this describe your relationship with God?

☑ How can you apply this scripture to your life?

☑ What changes do you need to make?

☑ Who needs to hear this scripture?

Day 21

Honor the laws of the Eternal your God, and live by His truth. Be faithful to His laws, commands, judgments, and precepts —the ones written for us in the instructions of Moses. If you follow this path, you will be successful in everything you do no matter where you are.

1 Kings 2:3 (VOICE)

Day 21
Firestarter
Fuel for Fire: *Faith*

☑ Who wrote this scripture and what were the circumstances?

☑ How do you see faith and faithfulness connected in this scripture?

☑ Describe this passage in your own words.

☑ What do you find difficult with this passage? How does it relate to your faith?

☑ Who needs to hear this scripture?

Day 22

For the word of the Lord is upright,
And all His work is *done* in faithfulness.

Psalm 33:4 (NASB)

Day 22
Firestarter
Fuel for Fire: *Faith*

☑ What does "the word of the Lord is upright" mean?

☑ How has God done "all His work in faithfulness"? How does this challenge your own work and faith?

☑ Describe your faith in God's word?

☑ How can you apply this scripture to your life?

☑ What changes do you need to make?

☑ Who needs to hear this scripture?

Day 23

³ Trust in the Lord and do good;
Dwell in the land and cultivate faithfulness.

Psalm 37:3 (NASB)

Day 23
Firestarter
Fuel for Fire: *Faith*

☑ Write out this passage in your own words.

☑ How does a person cultivate faith? How are you cultivating your faith?

☑ Find another passage in the bible that further explains this scripture.

☑ Why should we trust in God? How does trusting God help our faith?

☑ Who needs to hear this scripture?

Day 24

5 For the Lord is good;
His lovingkindness is everlasting
And His faithfulness to all generations.

Psalm 100:5 (NASB)

Day 24
Firestarter
Fuel for Fire: *Faith*

☑ How does this scripture challenge your faith?

☑ Why is this passage important?

☑ What is God promising in this passage?

☑ Who needs to hear this scripture?

Day 25

6 My eyes shall be upon the faithful of the
land, that they may dwell with me;
He who walks in a blameless way is the
one who will minister to me.

Psalm 101:6 (NASB)

Day 25
Firestarter
Fuel for Fire: *Faith*

☑ What does this scripture teach you about having faith in God?

☑ How do you see yourself in this scripture?

☑ Does this describe your relationship with God?

☑ Who needs to hear this scripture?

Day 26

30 I have chosen the faithful way;
I have placed Your ordinances *before me*.

Psalm 119:30 (NASB)

Day 26
Firestarter
Fuel for Fire: *Faith*

☑ Find other scriptures that further explain this passage. How do they connect to your faith?

☑ Write your version of this passage.

☑ According to this scripture, what does God expect from you regarding your faith?

☑ Who needs to hear this scripture?

Day 27

4 He is the Rock, his works are perfect,
and all his ways are just.
A faithful God who does no wrong,
upright and just is he.

Deuteronomy 32:4 (NIV)

Day 27
Firestarter
Fuel for Fire: *Faith*

☑ Why is this scripture meaningful to Christians?

☑ How can this passage help you grow in your faith?

☑ Where are you challenged in your faith regarding this passage?

☑ Who needs to hear this scripture?

Day 28

14 "Now fear the Lord and serve him with all faithfulness.

Joshua 24:14(a) (NIV)

Day 28
Firestarter
Fuel for Fire: *Faith*

☑ In practical terms, what does it mean to "fear the Lord"?

☑ In what ways does this passage describe your relationship with God?

☑ Explain how a person serves the Lord "with all faithfulness".

☑ How would you teach this passage to inspire someone else's faith?

☑ Who needs to hear this scripture?

Day 29

5 Your love, Lord, reaches to the heavens,
  your faithfulness to the skies.

Psalm 36:5 (NIV)

Day 29
Firestarter
Fuel for Fire: *Faith*

☑ How are love and faith connected in this scripture?

☑ How far away are the heavens? In what ways does this increase your faith in God?

☑ What other passages does this scripture remind you of?

☑ This passage praises God. How can praising God build your faith in Him?

☑ Who needs to hear this scripture?

Day 30

19 Then he said to him, "Rise and go; your faith has made you well."

Luke 17:19 (NIV)

Day 30
Firestarter
Fuel for Fire: *Faith*

☑ Read Luke 17:11-19. What is this scripture trying to teach you?

☑ How does this scripture describe your faith in God?

☑ Would other people say that this scripture reminds them of your walk with God? How?

☑ Who needs to hear this scripture?

Day 31

²⁴ He was a good man, full of the Holy Spirit and faith, and a great number of people were brought to the Lord.

Acts 11:24 NIV)

Day 31
Firestarter
Fuel for Fire: *Faith*

☑ Who is this passage referring to? Why is it important for our understanding of faith?

☑ How do you see yourself in this scripture?

☑ Who are you sharing your faith with today? How?

☑ How can you apply this scripture to your life?

☑ What changes do you need to make?

☑ Who needs to hear this scripture?

Strength

~

Judges 6 & 7

Day 32

²⁹ God strengthens the weary
and gives vitality to those worn down *by
age and care.*

Isaiah 40:29 (VOICE)

Day 32
Firestarter
Fuel for Fire: *Strength*

☑ Describe physical and spiritual strength?

☑ Our strength comes from God. How has He been giving you strength?

☑ In which areas of your life do you need some additional spiritual strength?

☑ Write out the passage in your own words.

☑ How can you apply this scripture to your life?

☑ Who needs to hear this scripture?

Day 33

30 You should love the Eternal, your God, with all your heart, with all your soul, with all your mind, and with all your strength."

Mark 12:30 (VOICE)

Day 33
Firestarter
Fuel for Fire: *Strength*

- ☑ This scripture is well known. How does a person live this out practically?

- ☑ It says "You should" love God. What are the implications on your strength if you choose not to?

- ☑ How can you love the family of God with all your strength? Why should you?

- ☑ Would other people say that this scripture reminds them of your walk with God?

- ☑ Who needs to hear this scripture?

Day 34

But I have prayed for you. I have prayed
that your faith will hold firm and that you
will recover from your failure and become a
source of strength for your brothers here.

Luke 22:32 (VOICE)

Day 34
Firestarter
Fuel for Fire: *Strength*

- ☑ What is the connection between God, prayer and strength?

- ☑ What is the story behind this scripture?

- ☑ How are you a source of strength for others?

- ☑ Where do you need to grow in your spiritual strength? What is your plan?

- ☑ Who needs to hear this scripture?

Day 35

²² In each place, they brought strength to the disciples, encouraging them to remain true to the faith.

Acts 14:22(a) (VOICE)

Day 35
Firestarter
Fuel for Fire: *Strength*

☑ What is this scripture trying to teach you?

☑ How are you challenged by this passage?

☑ Why is this scripture important to you?
How does it help your understanding of
spiritual strength?

☑ How can you apply this scripture to your
life?

☑ Who needs to hear this scripture?

Day 36

5 The churches were strengthened in the faith by their visit and kept growing in numbers on a daily basis.

Acts 16:5 (VOICE)

Day 36
Firestarter
Fuel for Fire: *Strength*

- ☑ How are you strengthening your church today?

- ☑ When was the last time you helped strengthen a non-Christian in their knowledge of God? What changes should you make?

- ☑ Which churches have you visited? How does this build strength for you and other people?

- ☑ Who needs to hear this scripture?

Day 37

2 "The Lord is my strength and song,
And He has become my salvation;
This is my God, and I will praise Him;
My father's God, and I will extol Him.

Exodus 15:2 (NASB)

Day 37
Firestarter
Fuel for Fire: *Strength*

☑ What are the main points of the passage?

☑ How do your life experiences impact your relationship with God?

☑ What is the history behind this scripture? Why is it important?

☑ Who needs to hear this scripture?

Day 38

11 I am still as strong today as I was in the day Moses sent me; as my strength was then, so my strength is now, for war and for going out and coming in.

Joshua 14:11 (NASB)

Day 38
Firestarter
Fuel for Fire: *Strength*

- ☑ Rewrite this passage according to your own spiritual journey. How has God strengthened you?

- ☑ What battles do you need God's strength to overcome?

- ☑ Does this passage describe your relationship with God?

- ☑ What changes do you need to make?

- ☑ Who needs to hear this scripture?

Day 39

14 The Lord looked at him and said, "Go in this your strength and deliver Israel from the hand of Midian. Have I not sent you?"

Judges 6:14 (NASB)

Day 39
Firestarter
Fuel for Fire: *Strength*

☑ What is the writer explaining about God here?

☑ How do you see yourself in this scripture?

☑ Where does God want you to take His strength today?

☑ Who do you need to "deliver" or help in their relationship with God?

☑ Who needs to hear this scripture?

Day 40

¹¹ Seek the Lord and His strength;
Seek His face continually.

1 Chronicles 16:11 (NASB)

Day 40
Firestarter
Fuel for Fire: *Strength*

☑ Why is this scripture important?

☑ How do you get strength from the Lord?

☑ What does it mean to "Seek His face continually"?

☑ Who needs to hear this scripture?

Day 41

²⁷ Splendor and majesty are before Him,
Strength and joy are in His place.

1 Chronicles 16:27 (NASB)

Day 41
Firestarter
Fuel for Fire: *Strength*

- ☑ What is this scripture trying to teach you?

- ☑ Where do you see yourself in this scripture?

- ☑ How can you apply this scripture to your life?

- ☑ What changes do you need to make?

- ☑ Who needs to hear this scripture?

Day 42

⁸ Observe therefore all the commands I am giving you today, so that you may have the strength to go in and take over the land that you are crossing the Jordan to possess.

Deuteronomy 11:8 (NIV)

Day 42
Firestarter
Fuel for Fire: *Strength*

☑ Read the entire chapter, Deuteronomy 11. What can you learn from this chapter?

☑ How does this scripture call you higher?

☑ Who do you know in your church that reminds you of this a passage? How?

☑ How can you apply this scripture to your life?

☑ What changes do you need to make?

☑ Who needs to hear this scripture?

Day 43

7 Moses was a hundred and twenty years old when he died, yet his eyes were not weak nor his strength gone.

Deuteronomy 34:7 (NIV)

Day 43
Firestarter
Fuel for Fire: *Strength*

☑ Why is this scripture important? How does it relate to God's strength in your life?

☑ Does this describe your relationship with God? Why or why not?

☑ Compare your life to Moses' - What are the similarities? Differences?

☑ Who needs to hear this scripture?

Day 44

16 And Saul's son Jonathan went to David at Horesh and helped him find strength in God.

1 Samuel 23:16 (NIV)

Day 44
Firestarter
Fuel for Fire: *Strength*

☑ In your own words, write down the importance of Jonathan and David's friendship.

☑ Write down the names of people that are close to you in your church. How are you strengthening each other?

☑ Does this describe your relationship with God? Other Christians?

☑ What changes do you need to make?

☑ Who needs to hear this scripture?

Day 45

33 It is God who arms me with strength and keeps my way secure.

2 Samuel 22:33 (NIV)

Day 45
Firestarter
Fuel for Fire: *Strength*

☑ How do you see yourself in this scripture?

☑ Does this describe your relationship with God? What next steps should you take to strengthen your relationship with God?

☑ How have you relied on God's strength? What was the outcome?

☑ Who needs to hear this scripture?

Day 46

⁴⁰ You armed me with strength for battle;
you humbled my adversaries before me.

2 Samuel 22:40 (NIV)

Day 46
Firestarter
Fuel for Fire: *Strength*

☑ Write out a modern version of this passage.
What is this scripture trying to teach you?

☑ Who are your adversaries? How should you
protect yourself from them?

☑ What is the historical context of this
passage?

☑ Who needs to hear this scripture?

Perseverance

~

Numbers 14:1-38

Day 47

16 Pay close attention to yourself and to your teaching; persevere in these things, for as you do this you will ensure salvation both for yourself and for those who hear you.

1 Timothy 4:16 (NASB)

Day 47
Firestarter
Fuel for Fire: *Perseverance*

- ☑ How would you explain this passage to another person?

- ☑ What does perseverance look like practically?

- ☑ How is perseverance important in life? In relationships? With God?

- ☑ How can you apply this scripture to your life?

- ☑ What changes do you need to make?

- ☑ Who needs to hear this scripture?

Day 48

12 Blessed is a man who perseveres under trial; for once he has been approved, he will receive the crown of life which *the Lord* has promised to those who love Him.

James 1:12 (NASB)

Day 48
Firestarter
Fuel for Fire: *Perseverance*

☑ What are some trials you have experienced in life?

☑ How is a person "approved" by God?

☑ What trials are you in currently? Where do you need to persevere and why?

☑ Who was James writing to and what were the circumstances?

☑ Who needs to hear this scripture?

Day 49

⁶ Love does not delight in evil but rejoices with the truth. ⁷ It always protects, always trusts, always hopes, always perseveres.

1 Corinthians 13:6-7 (NIV)

Day 49
Firestarter
Fuel for Fire: *Perseverance*

☑ How would you describe the relationship between love and perseverance?

☑ What is this scripture trying to teach you?

☑ In what ways does this describe your relationship with God?

☑ How can you apply this scripture to your life?

☑ Who needs to hear this scripture?

Day 50

36 You need to persevere so that when you have done the will of God, you will receive what he has promised.

Hebrews 10:36 (NIV)

Day 50
Firestarter
Fuel for Fire: *Perseverance*

☑ What is the goal of your perseverance?

☑ Why is this passage important to know?

☑ What is the "will of God"? Write down some scriptures to answer this.

☑ Who needs to hear this scripture?

Day 51

²⁷ By faith he left Egypt, not fearing the king's anger; he persevered because he saw him who is invisible.

Hebrews 11:27 (NIV)

Day 51
Firestarter
Fuel for Fire: *Perseverance*

☑ Who is the writer talking about? What lessons can be learned about perseverance from his life?

☑ Who in your life is an example of perseverance? What is their story?

☑ How would you summarize Hebrews chapter 11? What challenges you to persevere?

☑ Who needs to hear this scripture?

Day 51

¹¹ As you know, we count as blessed those who have persevered. You have heard of Job's perseverance and have seen what the Lord finally brought about. The Lord is full of compassion and mercy.

James 5:11 (NIV)

Day 51
Firestarter
Fuel for Fire: *Perseverance*

- ☑ What is Job's story of perseverance? Why did James mention his story?

- ☑ What is the connection between God's compassion, His mercy and perseverance?

- ☑ How can you apply this scripture to your life?

- ☑ What changes do you need to make?

- ☑ Who needs to hear this scripture?

Day 52

³ You have persevered and have endured hardships for my name, and have not grown weary.

Day 52
Firestarter
Fuel for Fire: *Perseverance*

☑ How does this passage relate to your life? What are the hardships that you've endured for God?

☑ What next steps should you take to persevere in your trials?

☑ How does the story of your life encourage others to persevere? Do people know your story?

☑ Who needs to hear this scripture?

Day 53

4 But as God's servants, we commend ourselves in every situation. So that with great endurance we persevere even in anguish and hardship.

2 Corinthians 6:4(a)(VOICE)

Day 53
Firestarter
Fuel for Fire: *Perseverance*

☑ Write out this passage in your own words. What does God want you to know?

☑ Is it possible to persevere alone? Why or why not?

☑ What are the benefits of being a Christian when it comes to the trials of life?

☑ Who needs to hear this scripture?

Day 54

⁴ So, *of course,* we've proudly bragged about you *within circles of God's people* at other churches *near and far* because, even in *the grip of* much persecution and affliction, you've stood firm in your faith and have persevered.

2 Thessalonians 1:4 (VOICE)

Day 54
Firestarter
Fuel for Fire: *Perseverance*

☑ Who is this scripture about? What is their story?

☑ Who are you proud of in your church community? Who has an amazing story of perseverance?

☑ What inspires you about this passage?

☑ Who needs to hear this scripture?

Day 55

11 Look, we bless and honor the memory of those who persevered *under hardship.* Remember how Job endured and how the Lord orchestrated the triumph of his final circumstances as a grand display of His mercy and compassion.

James 5:11 (VOICE)

Day 55
Firestarter
Fuel for Fire: *Perseverance*

☑ We sometimes forget those who have passed on. Who has inspired your faith and moved you to persevere? How did their life matter to you?

☑ How would you like to be remembered? Write out your story as if someone was sharing at your funeral?

☑ How is God connected to Job's story? How is God connected to your story?

☑ Who needs to hear this scripture?

Day 56

¹⁹ Once you spoke in a vision,
to your faithful people you said:
"I have bestowed strength on a warrior;
I have raised up a young man from among
the people.

Psalm 89:19 (NIV)

Day 56
Firestarter
Fuel for Fire: *Perseverance*

☑ What is this story about and how does it relate to perseverance?

☑ What is the difference between perseverance and endurance?

☑ How has God raised you up? How have you limited God in shaping you?

☑ What is God's vision for your life? The lives of people around you?

☑ Who needs to hear this scripture?

Endurance

~

Luke 22:1-71

Day 57

³ Suffer hardship with *me*, as a good soldier of Christ Jesus.

2 Timothy 2:3 (NASB)

Day 57
Firestarter
Fuel for Fire: *Endurance*

☑ Describe how Jesus is the ultimate example of endurance.

☑ Write down how you've endured as a Christian. How does this make you feel about yourself?

☑ Why do Christians need to suffer in their walk with God?

☑ How can you apply this scripture to your life?

☑ Who needs to hear this scripture?

Day 58

23 If you do this thing and
God *so* commands you, then you will be
able to endure.

Exodus 18:23(a) (NASB)

Day 58
Firestarter
Fuel for Fire: *Endurance*

☑ What is the writer trying to explain here regarding endurance?

☑ What commands of God do you find most difficult to follow? Why?

☑ What is your favorite passage on endurance? How does this passage inspire you?

☑ Who needs to hear this scripture?

Day 59

31 Let the glory of the Lord endure forever;
Let the Lord be glad in His works.

Psalm 104:31 (NASB)

Day 59
Firestarter
Fuel for Fire: *Endurance*

☑ Is God the central character in your story of endurance? Why or why not?

☑ How do you see yourself in this scripture?

☑ What is the Lord's glory? What is the connection with endurance?

☑ How can you make this scripture come alive in your life?

☑ Who needs to hear this scripture?

Day 60

³ Splendid and majestic is His work,
And His righteousness endures forever.

Psalm 111:3 (NASB)

Day 60
Firestarter
Fuel for Fire: *Endurance*

☑ How do you see yourself in this scripture?

☑ How would you explain this passage to a new believer?

☑ How does this passage oppose the world's idea of endurance and God?

☑ Who needs to hear this scripture?

Day 61

³ Wealth and riches are in his house,
And his righteousness endures forever.

Psalm 112:3 (NASB)

Day 61
Firestarter
Fuel for Fire: *Endurance*

☑ What encourages you about this passage?

☑ What new insights can you make about God?

☑ What are "Wealth and riches" according to God? Find other passages to answer this question.

☑ Who needs to hear this scripture?

Day 62

27 Do not work for food that spoils, but for food that endures to eternal life, which the Son of Man will give you.

John 6:27(a) (NIV)

Day 62
Firestarter
Fuel for Fire: *Endurance*

☑ How are you working for God today?
Would He be proud of you?

☑ What work in your life is pulling you away
from God? Why?

☑ What do you believe is the work that God
wants you to do for Him? What are your
plans to accomplish the work?

☑ Who needs to hear this scripture?

Day 63

¹² We work hard with our own hands. When we are cursed, we bless; when we are persecuted, we endure it.

1 Corinthians 4:12 (NIV)

Day 63
Firestarter
Fuel for Fire: *Endurance*

☑ Why is this passage important for you to know?

☑ How is being persecuted a good thing? What are the benefits for you and other people?

☑ Does this describe your relationship with God? How?

☑ Who needs to hear this scripture?

Day 64

13 No temptation has overtaken you except what is common to mankind. And God is faithful; he will not let you be tempted beyond what you can bear. But when you are tempted, he will also provide a way out so that you can endure it.

1 Corinthians 10:13 (NIV)

Day 64
Firestarter
Fuel for Fire: *Endurance*

☑ What are your temptations? Who do share your struggles with?

☑ What are some practical ways you can escape from being tempted and sinning?

☑ What is the connection between temptation and endurance?

☑ Who needs to hear this scripture?

Day 65

[12] if we endure,
we will also reign with him.
If we disown him,
he will also disown us.

2 Timothy 2:12 (NIV)

Day 65
Firestarter
Fuel for Fire: *Endurance*

☑ How does this passage make you feel about God?

☑ How have you disowned God? What changes do you need to make?

☑ What does it mean to "reign with him"?

☑ How can you apply this scripture to your life?

☑ Who needs to hear this scripture?

Day 66

³ Consider him who endured such opposition from sinners, so that you will not grow weary and lose heart.

Hebrews 12:3 (NIV)

Day 66
Firestarter
Fuel for Fire: *Endurance*

☑ In a few sentences, write out your version of Jesus' life and mission.

☑ What opposition did Jesus endure? Why is this relevant to your spiritual life?

☑ How have you become weary? What help do you need?

☑ How can you apply this scripture to your life?

☑ Who needs to hear this scripture?

Day 67

⁷ Endure hardship as discipline; God is treating you as his children. For what children are not disciplined by their father?

Hebrews 12:7 (NIV)

Day 67
Firestarter
Fuel for Fire: *Endurance*

☑ What is this scripture trying to teach you?

☑ How has God's discipline helped you?

☑ How have you rejected God's discipline?
   Why?

☑ How has your past impacted your thoughts
   about God? What is the truth about God's
   love? Find some passages and write them
   down.

☑ Who needs to hear this scripture?

Day 68

90 Your faithfulness endures to every
generation;
You founded the earth, and it remains.

Psalm 119:90 (VOICE)

Day 68
Firestarter
Fuel for Fire: *Endurance*

☑ What is the significance of this passage?

☑ How does this passage challenge you to be more like God?

☑ How are you passing on the knowledge of God to the next generation? Can you do anything better?

☑ Who needs to hear this scripture?

Day 69

21 For those who live right will remain in the land
and those with integrity will endure here.

Proverbs 2:21 (VOICE)

Day 69
Firestarter
Fuel for Fire: *Endurance*

- ☑ How does this scripture relate to your life today?

- ☑ What is integrity? Why is integrity important as a follower of Jesus?

- ☑ Why does God give people so many scriptures to follow? What is His purpose?

- ☑ How would you share this passage to encourage someone? What would you say are the key ideas?

- ☑ Who needs to hear this scripture?

Day 70

14 The human spirit can endure *a
long* illness,
but who can survive a crushed spirit?

Proverbs 18:14 (VOICE)

Day 70
Firestarter
Fuel for Fire: *Endurance*

☑ Explain this scripture by using some real life examples.

☑ Where do you see yourself in this scripture?

☑ What is a crushed spirit? Why can a person not survive a crushed spirit?

☑ How can a person avoid a crushed spirit?

☑ Who needs to hear this scripture?

Day 71

2 Where there is rebellion in a land,
there are many *petty and
contending* rulers;
But where there is a wise and intelligent
leader,
peace and order endure.

Proverbs 28:2 (VOICE)

Day 71
Firestarter
Fuel for Fire: *Endurance*

☑ Re-write this passage in your own words.
What can you learn from this scripture?

☑ Where are the rebellions in society today?

☑ What role should we play as Christians in
society? Why?

☑ How does wisdom connect with
endurance? Explain.

☑ Who needs to hear this scripture?

Day 72

14 I know everything God does endures for all time. Nothing can be added to it; nothing can be taken away from it. We humans can only stand in awe of all God has done.

Ecclesiastes 3:14 (VOICE)

Day 72
Firestarter
Fuel for Fire: *Endurance*

☑ What does this scripture teach you about God's plans and His endurance?

☑ You are part of God's new creation as a Christian. In light of this, how does this passage make you feel about your relationship with Him?

☑ What does this passage teach about the connection between your endurance as a Christian and praising God?

☑ Who needs to hear this scripture?

Love

~

Deuteronomy 4:32-40

Day 73

2 He said, "Take now your son, your only son, whom you love, Isaac, and go to the land of Moriah, and offer him there as a burnt offering on one of the mountains of which I will tell you."

Genesis 22:2 (NASB)

Day 73
Firestarter
Fuel for Fire: *Love*

☑ What is this story about? How is the love of God a central theme?

☑ Where do you see yourself in this scripture?

☑ How would you feel if you were Abraham? How does this instruction of God challenge your understanding of God's love for you?

☑ Who needs to hear this scripture?

Day 74

¹⁸ You shall not take vengeance, nor bear any grudge against the sons of your people, but you shall love your neighbor as yourself; I am the Lord.

Leviticus 19:18 (NASB)

Day 74
Firestarter
Fuel for Fire: *Love*

☑ How do you love your neighbor? Write down the ways God expects us to love other people. Use additional scriptures to explain your answer.

☑ Why is the statement "I am the Lord" the key element of the passage? Where do you see yourself in this scripture?

☑ Write down the names of your neighbors that you love like this. What next steps will you take to love them as God intended?

☑ Who needs to hear this scripture?

Day 75

9 You shall not worship them or serve them; for I, the Lord your God, am a jealous God, visiting the iniquity of the fathers on the children, and on the third and the fourth *generations* of those who hate Me, 10 but showing lovingkindness to thousands, to those who love Me and keep My commandments.

Deuteronomy 5:9-10 (NASB)

Day 75
Firestarter
Fuel for Fire: *Love*

☑ What is the context behind the passage?

☑ Write out this passage in your own words?

☑ What is hatred towards God? Find other
   scriptures that help to understand this idea.

☑ Who needs to hear this scripture?

Day 76

⁵ You shall love the Lord your God with all your heart and with all your soul and with all your might.

Deuteronomy 6:5 (NASB)

Day 76
Firestarter
Fuel for Fire: *Love*

☑ Describe, heart, soul and might as they relate to this command.

☑ How does a person practically live out this passage?

☑ How can you apply this scripture to your life?

☑ What changes do you need to make?

☑ Who needs to hear this scripture?

Day 77

¹¹ But let all who take refuge in You be
glad,
Let them ever sing for joy;
And may You shelter them,
That those who love Your name may exult
in You.

Psalm 5:11 (NASB)

Day 77
Firestarter
Fuel for Fire: *Love*

☑ How would you describe your love for God to someone else?

☑ What does it mean to "take refuge" in God?

☑ Are you happy in your relationship with God? What next steps will you take to improve the relationship?

☑ Who needs to hear this scripture?

Day 78

22 "How long will you who are simple love
your simple ways?
How long will mockers delight in mockery
and fools hate knowledge?

Proverbs 1:22 (NIV)

Day 78
Firestarter
Fuel for Fire: *Love*

☑ How do you see yourself in this scripture?

☑ Describe "simple ways" and "mockery". How do they relate to God's love for you and your love for Him?

☑ What does it mean to "hate knowledge"?

☑ Who needs to hear this scripture?

Day 79

³ Let love and faithfulness never leave you;
bind them around your neck,
write them on the tablet of your heart.

Proverbs 3:3 (NIV)

Day 79
Firestarter
Fuel for Fire: *Love*

- ☑ Who wrote this scripture and why is it important for you to understand?

- ☑ How can you lose "love and faithfulness"? How do you see yourself in this scripture?

- ☑ Write down some practical changes you need to make in order to grow in your "love and faithfulness". Commit to prayers.

- ☑ Who needs to hear this scripture?

Day 80

6 Do not forsake wisdom, and she will protect you;
love her, and she will watch over you.

Proverbs 4:6 (NIV)

Day 80
Firestarter
Fuel for Fire: *Love*

☑ What "wisdom" is the writer talking about? How is wisdom important?

☑ Write down the times in your life when you lived like this scripture. How did you feel about God's love?

☑ How does this passage help you to love other people?

☑ Who needs to hear this scripture?

Day 81

¹⁷ A friend loves at all times,
and a brother is born for a time of
adversity.

Proverbs 17:17 (NIV)

Day 81
Firestarter
Fuel for Fire: *Love*

☑ What is another way you could explain this passage to someone?

☑ How does this passage challenge your love for other people?

☑ What are the benefits of living your life this way?

☑ Who needs to hear this scripture?

Day 82

⁹ The Lord detests the way of the wicked,
but he loves those who pursue
righteousness.

Proverbs 15:9 (NIV)

Day 82
Firestarter
Fuel for Fire: *Love*

☑ How does this passage help you understand God's love? His mercy and grace?

☑ What does it mean to detest something? How should this motivate you to change spiritually?

☑ Does God expect you to be perfect according to this scripture? Why or why not?

☑ Who needs to hear this scripture?

Day 83

44 But I tell you this: love your enemies. Pray for those who torment you and persecute you.

Matthew 5:44 (VOICE)

Day 83
Firestarter
Fuel for Fire: *Love*

- ☑ What are the benefits of living your life this way? How would society change?

- ☑ How does the command challenge you?

- ☑ Who do you know who lives like this currently? What make them different from other people?

- ☑ Write down a list of the people you need to love this way. Write down the next steps to fulfill this scripture in your life.

- ☑ Who needs to hear this scripture?

Day 84

37 If you love your father or mother more than you love Me, then you are not worthy of Me. If you love your son or daughter more than you love Me, then you are not worthy of Me.

Matthew 10:37 (VOICE)

Day 84
Firestarter
Fuel for Fire: *Love*

☑ What is this scripture trying to teach you?

☑ Do you live this way right now? What improvements do you need to make to live this way?

☑ How have your life experiences impacted your understanding of this passage?

☑ Who needs to hear this scripture?

Day 85

32 Listen, what's the big deal if you love people who already love you? Even scoundrels do that much!

Luke 6:32 (VOICE)

Day 85
Firestarter
Fuel for Fire: *Love*

☑ Read Luke 6:27-36.

☑ What is this scripture trying to teach you about your love for God and other people?

☑ Go through the passage again. Write down the opposite of each command. How does this help you understand God's love?

☑ Who needs to hear this scripture?

Day 86

43 Woe to you, Pharisees! *Judgment will come on you!* What you really love is having people fawn over you when you take the seat of honor in the synagogue or when you are greeted in the public market.

Luke 11:43 (VOICE)

Day 86
Firestarter
Fuel for Fire: *Love*

☑ What is Jesus doing in this passage? How is He showing love for the Pharisees?

☑ How does God show His love for people?

☑ How do you see yourself in the story?

☑ How can you apply this scripture to your life?

☑ Who needs to hear this scripture?

Day 87

¹⁷ As the impact of His words settled in, His critics were humiliated, but everyone else loved what Jesus said and celebrated everything He was doing.

Luke 13:17 (VOICE)

Day 87
Firestarter
Fuel for Fire: *Love*

☑ What is the contrast being taught in this scripture? How does it apply to the Christian life?

☑ What does it mean to be humiliated? Describe a time you felt this way.

☑ How can humiliation lead a person to love God?

☑ When was the last time you held a celebration for God's work in your life? What are your plans to celebrate Him in the future?

☑ Who needs to hear this scripture?

Testing

~

Matthew 4:1-11

Day 88

Eternal One *(to Moses)*: ⁴ Look! I will
cause bread to rain down from heaven
for you, and the people will go out and
gather a helping of it each day. I will test
them to see if they are willing to live by
My instructions.

Exodus 16:4 (VOICE)

Day 88
Firestarter
Fuel for Fire: *Testing*

☑ What is the story of this passage? How does it help you in your understanding of God?

☑ How does God test people?

☑ Why does God test people? How have you been tested?

☑ Who needs to hear this scripture?

Day 89

Moses: [20] Don't be afraid. These *powerful manifestations* are God's way of instilling *awe and* fear in you so that you will not sin; He is testing you *for your own good.*

Exodus 20:20 (VOICE)

Day 89
Firestarter
Fuel for Fire: *Testing*

☑ According to this scripture, how does God help protect people through testing?

☑ Why does God command people to not be afraid?

☑ Write down the connection between testing, faith and sin.

☑ Who needs to hear this scripture?

Day 90

2 Remember how the Eternal, your True God, led you through the wilderness these past 40 years. He did this to humble you, to test you, to uncover your motivations, to see if you would obey His commands.

Deuteronomy 8:2 (VOICE)

Day 90
Firestarter
Fuel for Fire: *Testing*

☑ What can you learn from this scripture?

☑ How has God humbled you? How did this help you?

☑ What are your motivations as a Christian? What changes should you make?

☑ Would other people say that this scripture reminds them of your walk with God? How?

☑ Who needs to hear this scripture?

Day 91

²² I will put My people to the test to see
 whether or not they will walk the faithful
 way of the Eternal as their ancestors did.

Judges 2:22 (VOICE)

Day 91
Firestarter
Fuel for Fire: *Testing*

☑ Using your life as the background, write out your version of this passage. How does this challenge you about God?

☑ Name some people that have inspired your faith. What testing did they go through?

☑ How is the book of Judges important to you and your relationship with God?

☑ Who needs to hear this scripture?

Day 92

¹⁷ O my God, You test the heart and delight
when it is proven faithful,
so I, with an honest heart, have willingly
offered all these things.
And now I have joyfully witnessed Your
people, who are present here,
make their offerings willingly *and*
joyously to You.

1 Chronicles 29:17 (VOICE)

Day 92
Firestarter
Fuel for Fire: *Testing*

☑ How does this passage relate to your church community right now? How are the hearts being tested?

☑ Does this describe your relationship with God? How?

☑ How can you help other Christians who are being tested? Non-Christians?

☑ Who needs to hear this scripture?

Day 93

12 Now if any man builds on the foundation with gold, silver, precious stones, wood, hay, straw, 13 each man's work will become evident; for the day will show it because it is *to be* revealed with fire, and the fire itself will test the quality of each man's work. 14 If any man's work which he has built on it remains, he will receive a reward.

1 Corinthians 3:12-14 (NASB)

Day 93
Firestarter
Fuel for Fire: *Testing*

☑ In what ways does this passage describe your relationship with God?

☑ What is the main point of this scripture? Find another scripture to further explain your answer.

☑ What is your current spiritual foundation built upon? Would your foundation stand through a storm?

☑ Who needs to hear this scripture?

Day 94

²² We have sent with them our brother, whom we have often tested and found diligent in many things.

2 Corinthians 8:22 (NASB)

Day 94
Firestarter
Fuel for Fire: *Testing*

☑ What is Paul trying to teach here?

☑ Where do you see yourself in this scripture?

☑ What does this scripture make you think about in your own life?

☑ What is your vision for your future?

☑ Who needs to hear this scripture?

Day 95

5 Test yourselves *to see* if you are in the faith; examine yourselves! Or do you not recognize this about yourselves, that Jesus Christ is in you—unless indeed you fail the test?

2 Corinthians 13:5 (NASB)

Day 95
Firestarter
Fuel for Fire: *Testing*

- ☑ How do you test yourself "to see if you are in the faith?"

- ☑ What tests have you failed in life? Why?

- ☑ What scares you about this scripture? What encourages you?

- ☑ How can you apply this scripture to your life?

- ☑ Who needs to hear this scripture?

Day 96

¹⁷ By faith Abraham, when he was tested, offered up Isaac, and he who had received the promises was offering up his only begotten *son.*

Hebrews 11:17 (NASB)

Day 96
Firestarter
Fuel for Fire: *Testing*

☑ How can Abraham's testing help you as a Christian?

☑ What things do you love that you would be willing to sacrifice for God? Why or why not?

☑ What does God promise will result from His testing? Find other scriptures for the answer.

☑ Who needs to hear this scripture?

Day 97

2 Consider it all joy, my brethren, when you encounter various trials, 3 knowing that the testing of your faith produces endurance. 4 And let endurance have *its* perfect result, so that you may be perfect and complete, lacking in nothing.

James 1:2-4 (NASB)

Day 97
Firestarter
Fuel for Fire: *Testing*

☑ How does James relate joy and testing in this passage?

☑ What areas in your spiritual life are you lacking? What steps will you take to change this?

☑ How does a Christian reach perfection? Is it even possible?

☑ Who needs to hear this scripture?

Day 98

³ Though you probe my heart,
though you examine me at night and test
me,
you will find that I have planned no evil;
my mouth has not transgressed.

Psalm 17:3 (NIV)

Day 98
Firestarter
Fuel for Fire: *Testing*

☑ What is the history behind this passage?

☑ What is in your heart that God is revealing through His testing?

☑ Does this describe your relationship with God? How?

☑ Who needs to hear this scripture?

Day 99

2 Test me, Lord, and try me,
examine my heart and my mind.

Psalm 26:2 (NIV)

Day 99
Firestarter
Fuel for Fire: *Testing*

☑ What is the difference between heart and mind? How does this help you to understand God?

☑ What challenges you about this passage?

☑ How does this passage remind you of Jesus? Other people in your life?

☑ Who needs to hear this scripture?

Day 100

¹⁰ For you, God, tested us;
   you refined us like silver.

Psalm 66:10 (NIV)

Day 100
Firestarter
Fuel for Fire: *Testing*

☑ How is silver refined? How does this relate to you and God?

☑ How can this passage motivate you to help other people when they are being tested?

☑ Why is the scripture important to new Christians? Older Christians?

☑ Who needs to hear this scripture?

About the Uncapped Series

This series was developed to help men connect or re-connect with God in ways they never have before. This being said, the series is applicable to any Christian, male or female, but the inspiration was to create a spiritual fire in the hearts of our brothers.

We believe that so many Christian men have settled in life and their potential as soldiers for God and His will for their lives. They believe that they are limited in both their talents and abilities and never venture beyond these false truths.

But we know better. God is ready to take you to places and victories beyond your imagination.

It's time to become Uncapped!

Uncapped is an experience unlike anything you've ever encountered. We don't believe in limitations. We believe in God's power.

When you begin this new adventure, leave the baggage of your past at the door.

Your doubts will be replaced with dreams.
Apathy will be replaced with action.
Insecurity will be replaced with inspiration.
Your life will be changed forever.

Get ready for the adventure!

Meet the Authors

CJ Tetley has been teaching, training and coaching people for over twenty years. He has a background as a freestyle skier, a corporate trainer and has a degree in Education. He has been a Christian for almost 20 years and has been married for 17 years. He and his wife, Melissa, have two boys and live in Toronto and serve as shepherds in the Toronto Church.

Mike Abrokwah is passionate about people and their endless potential. If there was a soundtrack to his life, it would go something like this: "I believe we can all flourish in unfavourable climates". He strives to live UNCAPPED and is happy to tag alongside anyone who wishes to do the same. He has been a Christian for over 25 years and has been married for 17 years. He and his wife, Damali, have three children. The Abrokwahs live in Toronto where Mike serves as Evangelist in the Toronto Church.

Find Us Online

uncapped.ca

uncappedevents@gmail.com

33600829R00142